# THE READER'S DIGEST
# KEYBOARD COURSE

## Learn to Play 100 Unforgettable Songs the Easy Way

**Reader's Digest**

THE READER'S DIGEST ASSOCIATION, INC.
Pleasantville, New York/Montreal

Copyright © 2005 The Reader's Digest Association, Inc.
Copyright © 2005 The Reader's Digest Association (Canada) Ltd.
Copyright © 2005 Reader's Digest Association Far East Ltd.
Philippine Copyright © 2005 Reader's Digest Association Far East Ltd.

ISBN 0-7621-0688-3

Previously published in 1991 as *The Easy Way to Play 100 Unforgettable Hits*

Printed in China
1 3 5 7 9 10 8 6 4 2

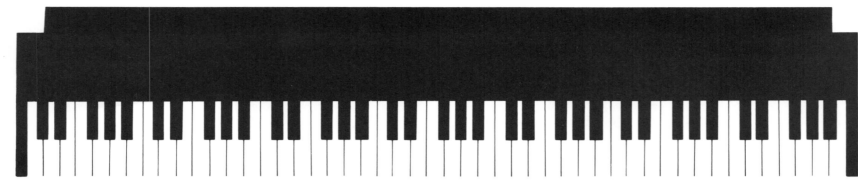

## Index to Sections

## Index to Songs

# How This Book Helps You to Play Real Music

We believe that anyone—well, *almost* anyone—can play music. And we believe that with this songbook, more people than ever before will be able to sit down and plunk out some of the best popular songs ever written.

THE READER'S DIGEST KEYBOARD COURSE has been designed primarily for two groups of people: those who have very limited piano skills and those who enjoy the electronic keyboard. If you play another instrument, you can use the book too, as you'll see when you read on. Whatever the instrument, everything is designed to let you play the melodies you know and love with the very least effort and with the utmost comfort and convenience.

To start with, there are the 100 melodies themselves. Every song in this book is, indeed, an unforgettable hit. All have been performed and recorded by many different stylists, both vocal and instrumental, and by different types of orchestras, from swing to sweet to symphonic. You'll find the glorious melodies and lyrics of such composers as George and Ira Gershwin, Richard Rogers and Oscar Hammerstein, Cole Porter,

Walter Donaldson, Jerome Kern, Alan Jay Lerner and Frederick Loewe, and Irving Berlin.

You will find just a few contemporary songs here. The reason for that is that many recent songs don't translate comfortably to a solo piano or keyboard: Their complex rhythms and bass guitar lines can't be duplicated without considerable effort, and the electronic effects that can be produced on a recording cannot be approximated. All of the songs here stand on their own as *melodies*.

The songs that we have included are songs that have endured, and will continue to endure, for generations. And all have been made easy—and fun—to play by Dan Fox, the master arranger of every Reader's Digest music book. All sound full and rich.

Now read on a bit, take a quick look at the few sample bars of "As Time Goes By" printed below and discover just how this book can work for you.

Keyboard players! Anything printed in blue is especially for you
Black print is for easy piano and more experienced players

## For Electronic Keyboards

Anything printed in blue is designed especially for you. This includes the top line of the music — the treble, or right-hand, clef — with the notes numbered for those who can't read music, as well as the suggested tempos, rhythms and colors (more about these later). Of course, if you can play the piano and use your electronic keyboard with both hands, just as you do an acoustic piano keyboard, it's advisable to play the full-scored piano arrangements for bass and treble clefs, printed in black. See the section on "Easy Piano" that follows for further information.

*For chords to accompany the melody*, look to the letters, also printed in blue, above the keyboard line. (The simplest, inexpensive monophonic [one-note-at-a-time] models of keyboard will not play chords.) For this and other instructions, *please consult the manual that came with your instrument.* The notes that can sound automatic chords will probably be identified on the backboard behind the keys of your instrument. But to help you find them, you can use the peel-off stickers with letter names that are provided with this book. (See "About the Stickers" on the following page.) You don't have to know what notes constitute each chord; just press the indicated key with your left hand. For a simple major chord you usually press one key or button. For example, to play a C chord, press a C in the designated bass portion of the keyboard, below Middle C. That

key will automatically play the three notes of a C chord (C, E and G). If you want a D chord (D-F♯-A), just press a D. To play minor chords or major and minor 7th chords (indicated in the music by such notations as Cm, G(7), Gm(7), and so on), you may have to use two, three or four fingers of your left hand. Different makes of keyboards require different techniques. For example, on a Casio, to play a minor chord, such as Cm, you play the C plus any neighboring note directly above the C. On a Yamaha, you would play the C plus any note *below* the C. If your instrument does not play 7th chords, you can still get a satisfactory harmony with the basic chord — say, a G rather than a G(7). In fact, the parentheses around the 7 indicate that the 7th chord is optional. *Again, consult your manual.*

At the top right-hand corner of the first page of each song, we have suggested tempos, rhythms and instrumental colors for that tune. Always remember that our suggestions are just that — *suggestions.* As you become more familiar with the keyboard, you'll begin to experiment with the music, and you'll have fun choosing your own instrumental sounds and different rhythms for a song.

*Counting time.* If you know how the song goes, you will probably know how long each note should be held — even if you don't know a half-note from a quarter-note. We don't go into musical notation here. However, we do show you where the beats are by the red marks underneath the lyrics; each mark ( ▾ ) is to be counted as one beat. Your electronic keyboard probably has a tempo light that blinks on each beat, so you can coordinate with that — one ▾ for each blink.

*Automatic rhythms.* The rhythms you can use on a song depend on the make and model of your instrument. Some electronic keyboards can play a polka rhythm; others cannot. Some have a "cha-cha" button, others a "bossa nova." Some can combine two rhythms to sound like a rhythm they don't have on a single button. Again, study your manufacturer's manual. And experiment.

*Instrumental colors.* Most keyboards offer piano, flute, guitar, strings, organ and a few other instrumental sounds, or colors. Some of the more versatile models allow you to mix different colors, which may enable you to come closer to the actual instrument sounds, or even to create your own sounds. Once again, consult your manual, since different makes offer different choices.

Once you know your keyboard and its many possibilities, you may be able to simulate an orchestral arrangement even if you are not a trained musician. Certainly your satisfaction will come easier and faster than you ever dared to dream, and you'll have great fun getting there. And remember, players on electronic instruments have a great advantage: you can play with earphones, and no one has to hear what you're doing until you're ready to turn on the amplifier and dazzle them.

## Easy Piano

Perhaps you're a piano student, or a retiree who is "getting back" to the piano after not touching it for most of your adult years. Or you're a wind instrument player who always wanted to "play a little piano." Then our very easy two-hand arrangements, printed in black, are for you. (The melody line, printed in blue, is for electronic keyboards.)

Since some players may have little experience with the bass, or left-hand, clef, our arrangements never ask you to play more than a single note at a time with your left hand. The name of each bass

note is printed in red under the lines, under each note. Until you grow more familiar with the bass notes, you can use the peel-off stickers to identify the notes in the two octaves from Middle C down. You might also find the beat marks ( ▾ ), printed in red, helpful.

More experienced players can refer to the chords that we've indicated at the top of the piano lines, in black. These chords are sometimes different from those on the keyboard, or blue, lines, substituting more complex harmonies that are not in the automatic chord bank of electronic keyboards.

## For Non-Keyboard Players

*If you play a single-note instrument,* such as a violin, flute, saxophone, clarinet, oboe, trumpet, harmonica or melodica, you can play from the electronic keyboard melody line (printed in blue), reading the notes. However, if you want to play in combination with another instrument, you would have to be sure that the other instrument is pitched in the same key. Clarinet, trumpet and tenor or soprano saxophone, for example, are B-flat instruments and can play together from the same music. Piano, guitar, accordion, autoharp, violin, flute, oboe and some recorders are in C. Alto and baritone saxophone and mellophone are in E flat, and so on.

*If you play accordion or autoharp,* you can certainly play from the blue lines; but depending on the options your particular instrument provides, you might get more variety out of the harmonies in the piano staves, printed in black. *Guitarists* can begin with the simpler chords of the blue lines and then graduate to the chords in black.

It's conceivable to us that different members of your household may use these arrangements in different ways at different levels of proficiency — the more the merrier.

Now, let's play the music! And perhaps you'd like to start with our musical illustration, the timeless "As Time Goes By." Go ahead, try it. See if Dooley Wilson, who played it in *Casablanca,* has anything on you. It's on page 108.

—*The Editors*

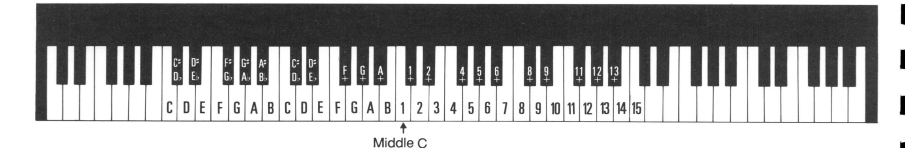

Middle C

## About the Stickers

A set of peel-off stickers for the keys of your piano or electronic keyboard is included with this book. The diagram above shows how to position them.

The numbered stickers are primarily for electronic keyboard players who can't read music. If you are in this category, you will be playing the top line of the music, printed in blue. These are the treble, or right-hand, notes.

The lettered stickers are for two octaves of notes in the bass, or left-hand, clef — to the left of Middle C — on both electronic keyboards and pianos.

To position the labels of the right-hand notes on your instrument, first find Middle C, which will be Number 1. It is in the center, or just to the left of center, of the keyboard, the first white key below the grouping of two black keys.

Then the black key directly up from C, or C sharp (C#) (which is the same as D flat [D♭]), becomes 1+. D becomes 2. D sharp (D#), the same as E flat (E♭), becomes 2+, and so on, following the diagram.

Notes in the bass clef are identified by their letter names rather than by numbers. Position them as shown on the diagram. Starting on the C two octaves below Middle C, the white keys will read C-D-E-F-G-A-B and repeat again up to 1 (Middle C). The black keys will read C#/D♭, D#/E♭, F#/G♭, G#/A♭, A#/B♭, until you reach the F#/G♭, G#/A♭ and A#/B♭ just to the left of Middle C. The stickers will identify these as F+, G+ and A+. The reason for this is that the melody sometimes reaches down to those keys below Middle C, and, for non-music-readers, this is consistent with the 1+, 2+ identifications of the melody from Middle C upward.

Words and Music by Johnny Mercer

Slow and steady          TEMPO: Moderate    RHYTHM: Rhumba, Bossa Nova    COLOR: Strings, Flute

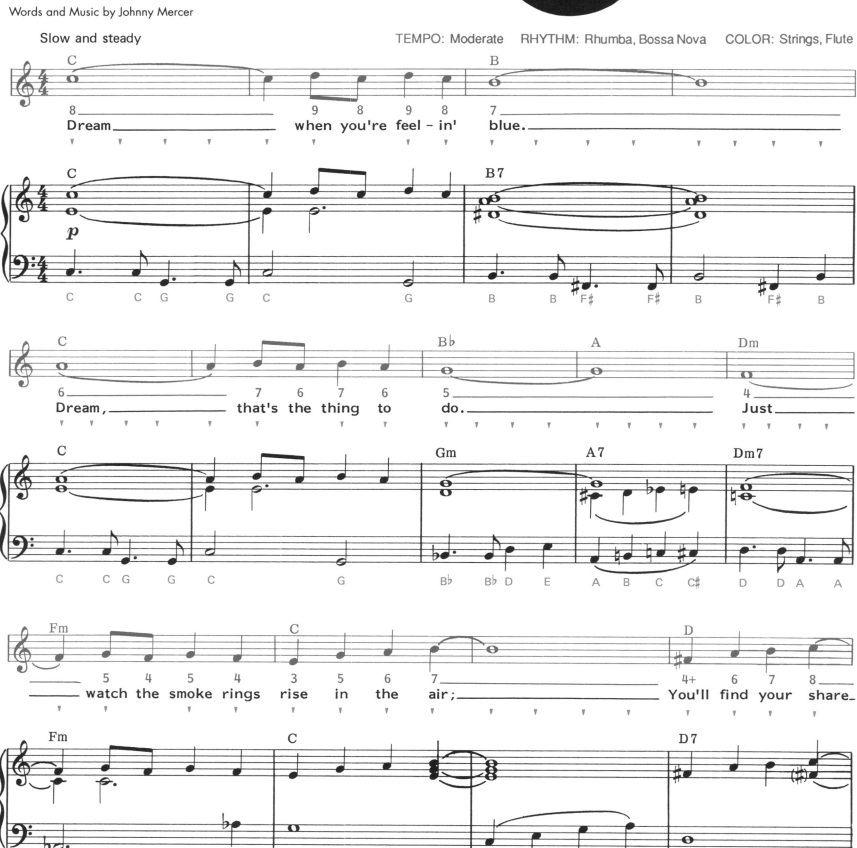

# Dream a Little Dream of Me

Words by Gus Kahn; Music by Wilbur Schwandt and Fabian Andre

TEMPO: Moderately slow    RHYTHM: Swing, Disco    COLOR: Vibraphone, Clarinet

# I Left My Heart in San Francisco

Words by Douglass Cross; Music by George Cory

TEMPO: Moderate    RHYTHM: Bossa Nova    COLOR: Electric Piano

# IN THE MOOD

Music by Joseph Garland

Lindy (♪♪ played as ♪³♪)     TEMPO: Moderate   RHYTHM: Swing, Big Band   COLOR: Reed ensemble, Sax or Brass ensemble

13

# LOVE LETTERS IN THE SAND

Words by Nick and Charles Kenny; Music by J. Fred Coots

TEMPO: Slow   RHYTHM: Rock   COLOR: Rock Guitar

# MISTY

Words by Johnny Burke; Music by Erroll Garner

TEMPO: Slow    RHYTHM: Slow Rock, Bossa Nova    COLOR: Jazz Organ, Strings

Words by Mitchell Parish; Music by Hoagy Carmichael

TEMPO: Slow   RHYTHM: Swing, Bossa Nova   COLOR: Flute, Strings

Star Dust
Chorus - in tempo, slowly

# SATIN DOLL

Words by Johnny Mercer;
Music by Duke Ellington and Billy Strayhorn

TEMPO: Moderately fast   RHYTHM: Swing, Big Band   COLOR: Jazz Organ, Piano

23

# Seems Like Old Times

Words and Music by Carmen Lombardo and John Jacob Loeb

TEMPO: Moderate   RHYTHM: Swing, Big Band   COLOR: Sax, Clarinet, Flute

# IT'S ALL IN THE GAME

Words by Carl Sigman; Music by Charles Gates Dawes

Moderately slow

TEMPO: Moderately slow   RHYTHM: Waltz   COLOR: Celeste, Vibraphone

# Too Young

Words by Sylvia Dee; Music by Sid Lippman

TEMPO: Moderate     RHYTHM: Big Band, Rhumba     COLOR: Vibraphone, Accordion

Words and Music by Bart Howard
TEMPO: Moderately slow   RHYTHM: Waltz   COLOR: Strings, Flute

# AUTUMN LEAVES

English words by Johnny Mercer; Music by Joseph Kosma    French words by Jacques Prévert

TEMPO: Moderate    RHYTHM: Rhumba, Bossa Nova    COLOR: Strings, Flute

# IT'S A SIN TO TELL A LIE

Words and Music by Billy Mayhew

TEMPO: Moderate   RHYTHM: Swing, Big Band   COLOR: Saxophone, Accordion

With a lilt

34

# I'm Gonna Sit Right Down and Write Myself a Letter

Words by Joe Young; Music by Fred E. Ahlert

Moderate swing

TEMPO: Moderate to Fast    RHYTHM: Swing, Big Band    COLOR: Jazz Organ, Honkytonk Piano, Guitar

# ALL OF ME

Words and Music by Seymour Simons and Gerald Marks

TEMPO: Moderate to Fast   RHYTHM: Swing, Big Band   COLOR: Brass ensemble

39

# Red Sails in the Sunset

Words by Jimmy Kennedy; Music by Hugh Williams

TEMPO: Moderate   RHYTHM: Rhumba, Slow Rock   COLOR: Strings, Flute, Harmonica

# The Very Thought of You

Words and Music by Ray Noble

TEMPO: Moderately slow   RHYTHM: Big Band, Swing   COLOR: Clarinet, Flute

Moderately slow, with a lilt

Lyrics:

The ver-y thought of you and I for-get to do the lit-tle or-di-na-ry things that ev-'ry-one ought to do.

I'm liv-ing in a kind of day-dream; I'm hap-py as a king. And fool-ish though it may seem, to me that's ev'ry-thing. The mere i-

# I Found a Million Dollar Baby

## (in a Five and Ten Cent Store)

Words by Billy Rose and Mort Dixon; Music by Harry Warren

TEMPO: Moderate   RHYTHM: Big Band, Swing   COLOR: Sax, Trombone

It was a luck-y A-pril show-er; It was the most con-ven-ient door;

I found a mil-lion dol-lar ba-by in a five and ten cent store.

The rain con-tin-ued for an hour; I hung a-round for three or four,

a-round a mil-lion dol-lar ba-by in a five and ten cent store. She was sell-ing

# These Foolish Things
### (Remind Me of You)

Words by Holt Marvell; Music by Jack Strachey and Harry Link.

TEMPO: Very slow   RHYTHM: Big Band, Swing   COLOR: Strings, Organ

# TENDERLY

Words by Jack Lawrence; Music by Walter Gross

TEMPO: Very slow   RHYTHM: Waltz   COLOR: Strings

Slow waltz

The eve-ning breeze ca-ressed the trees ten-der - ly._____ The trem-bling

trees em-braced the breeze ten-der - ly._____ Then

you and I came wan - der - ing by, and

lost in a sigh were we._____ The shore was

# FOOLS RUSH IN

Words by Johnny Mercer; Music by Rube Bloom

TEMPO: Moderate   RHYTHM: Rhumba (Beguine)   COLOR: Flute, Strings

# WHAT'S NEW?

Words by Johnny Burke; Music by Bob Haggart

TEMPO: Moderately slow    RHYTHM: Beguine, Big Band    COLOR: Trumpet, Strings

52

# You Go to My Head

Words by Haven Gillespie; Music by J. Fred Coots

TEMPO: Slow    RHYTHM: Rhumba, Bossa Nova    COLOR: Flute, Clarinet, Horn

# ALL THE THINGS YOU ARE

From *Very Warm for May*    Words by Oscar Hammerstein II; Music by Jerome Kern

TEMPO: Moderate to Fast    RHYTHM: Big Band, Bossa Nova    COLOR: Jazz Organ, Sax, Clarinet

# Embraceable You

From *Girl Crazy*    Words by Ira Gershwin; Music by George Gershwin

TEMPO: Slow   RHYTHM: Swing, Bossa Nova   COLOR: Strings, Sax

# Tea for Two

From *No, No, Nanette*  Words by Irving Caesar; Music by Vincent Youmans

TEMPO: Moderately slow  RHYTHM: Pops, Cha Cha  COLOR: Muted Trumpet

With a lilt

# NIGHT AND DAY

From *The Gay Divorce*    Words and Music by Cole Porter

TEMPO: Moderate    RHYTHM: Rhumba, Beguine    COLOR: Strings, Flute

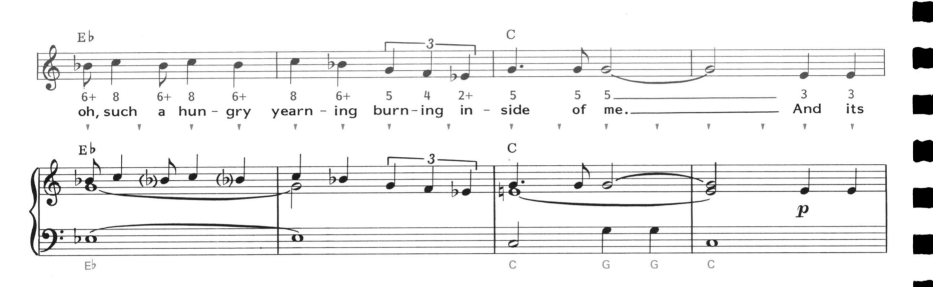

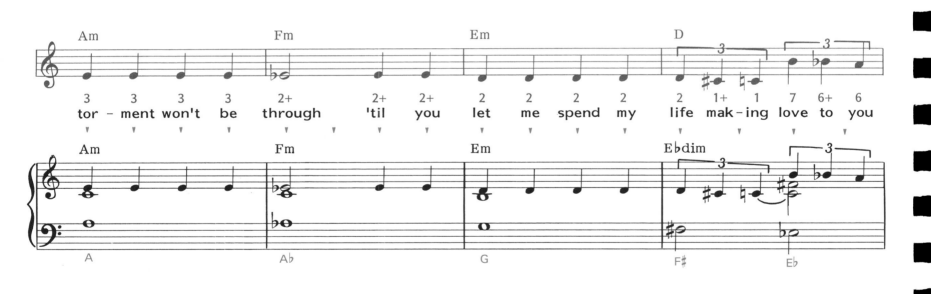

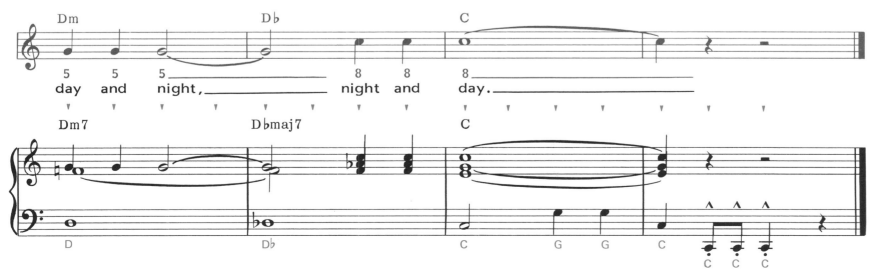

# I'VE GOT A CRUSH ON YOU

From *Treasure Girl* and *Strike Up the Band*    Words by Ira Gershwin; Music by George Gershwin

# April in Paris

From *Walk a Little Faster*

Words by E. Y. Harburg; Music by Vernon Duke

TEMPO: Slow to Moderate   RHYTHM: Swing  COLOR: Clarinet, Sax

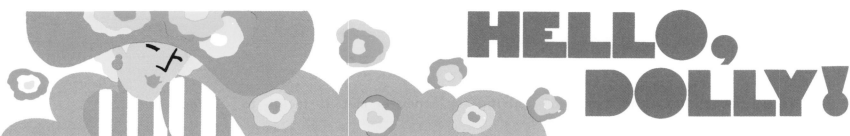

# HELLO, DOLLY!

*From Hello, Dolly!*     Words and Music by Jerry Herman

TEMPO: Fast   RHYTHM: Swing, Big Band   COLOR: Trumpet, Reed Synth.

# YOU DO SOMETHING TO ME

From *Fifty Million Frenchmen*

Words and Music by Cole Porter

TEMPO: Fast   RHYTHM: Swing   COLOR: Piano, Jazz Organ

Fast

# 'S Wonderful

From *Funny Face*   Words by Ira Gershwin; Music by George Gershwin

TEMPO: Moderately fast   RHYTHM: Swing, Big Band   COLOR: Jazz Organ, Trumpet

Moderately fast

Lyrics:
'S won-der-ful, 's mar-vel-ous, you should care for me. 's aw-ful nice, 's par-a-dise, 's what I love to see. You've

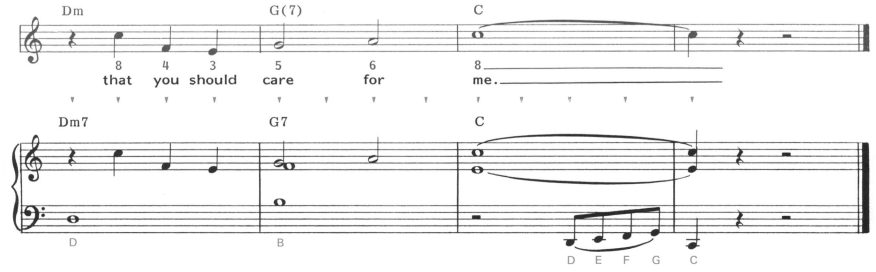

# The Man I Love

From *Strike Up the Band*       Words by Ira Gershwin; Music by George Gershwin

**Slowly**

TEMPO: Very slow       RHYTHM: Swing or Pops, or no rhythm       COLOR: Flute, Oboe, Accordion

Some-day he'll come a-long, the man I love; And he'll be big and strong, the man I love;

And when he comes my way, I'll do my best to make him stay.

He'll look at me and smile, I'll un-der-stand; And in a lit-tle while he'll take my hand;

And though it seems ab-surd, I know we both won't say a word.

# Dancing in the Dark

From *The Band Wagon*  Words by Howard Dietz; Music by Arthur Schwartz

TEMPO: Moderate   RHYTHM: Swing, Big Band   COLOR: Jazz Organ, Sax, Jazz Guitar

Copyright © 1931 (Renewed) Warner Bros. Inc. and Arthur Schwartz Publishing Designee. In Canada: Copyright © 1931 (Renewed) Warner Bros. Inc.

# DANCING ON THE CEILING

From *Ever Green*     Words by Lorenz Hart; Music by Richard Rodgers

TEMPO: Moderately slow     RHYTHM: Cha Cha, Pops     COLOR: Muted trumpet, Flute

# September Song

*From* Knickerbocker Holiday        Words by Maxwell Anderson; Music by Kurt Weill

Moderately slow

TEMPO: Moderately slow    RHYTHM: Bossa Nova or Beguine    COLOR: Cello

# Smoke Gets In Your Eyes

From *Roberta*     Words by Otto Harbach; Music by Jerome Kern

TEMPO: Slow   RHYTHM: None, play freely   COLOR: Strings

85

# With a Song in My Heart

From *Spring Is Here*  Words by Lorenz Hart; Music by Richard Rodgers

TEMPO: Moderate  RHYTHM: Rhumba, Big Band  COLOR: Flute, Strings

# My Heart Stood Still

From *A Connecticut Yankee*

Words by Lorenz Hart; Music by Richard Rodgers

TEMPO: Moderate   RHYTHM: Rhumba, Beguine   COLOR: Strings, Flute

# Love Me or Leave Me

From *Whoopee*  Words by Gus Kahn; Music by Walter Donaldson

TEMPO: Moderately fast  RHYTHM: Swing, Big Band  COLOR: Sax, Trombone

# LOVER, COME BACK TO ME

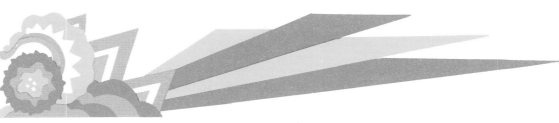

From *The New Moon*    Words by Oscar Hammerstein II; Music by Sigmund Romberg

TEMPO: Slow   RHYTHM: 16 Beat   COLOR: Strings

Slowly

The sky was blue and high a-bove; The moon was new, and so was love.

This ea-ger heart of mine was sing – ing, "Lov-er, where can you be?"

You came at last, love had its day; That day is past, you've gone a-way.

This ach-ing heart of mine is sing – ing, "Lov-er, come back to me." When

# Stouthearted Men

From *The New Moon*     Words by Oscar Hammerstein II; Music by Sigmund Romberg

March tempo     TEMPO: Moderate     RHYTHM: March; or manually strike chord note on every beat     COLOR: Trumpet

Give me some men who are stout-heart-ed men, who will fight for the right they a-dore.
Start me with ten who are stout-heart-ed men, and I'll soon give you ten thou-sand more. Oh!
Shoul-der to shoul-der and bold-er and bold-er they grow as they go to the fore.

# Someone to Watch Over Me

From *Oh, Kay!*    Words by Ira Gershwin; Music by George Gershwin

TEMPO: Slow   RHYTHM: Rhumba or Pops   COLOR: Flute or Strings

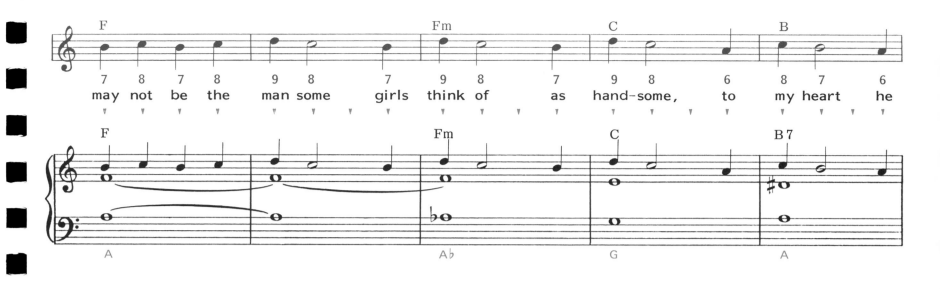

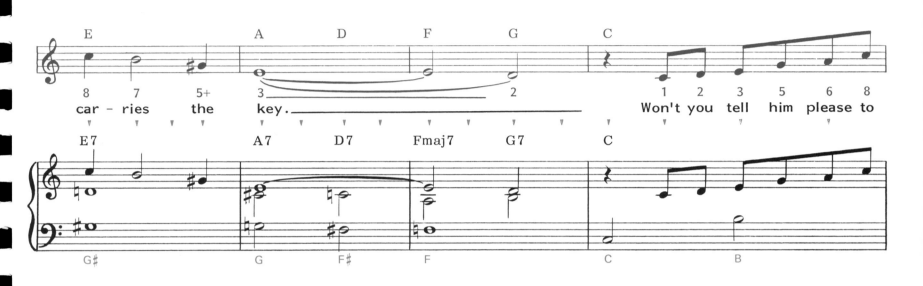

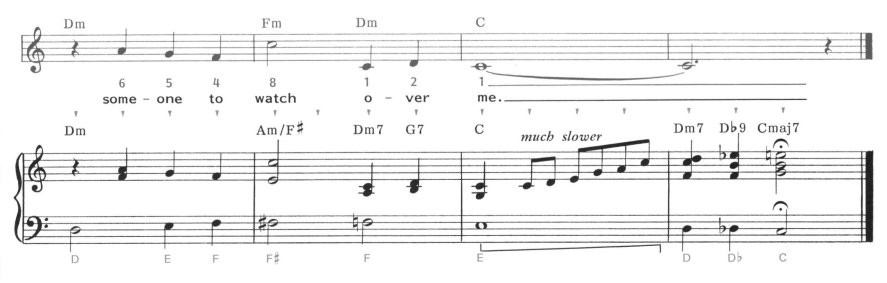

97

# SEND IN THE CLOWNS

From *A Little Night Music*    Words and Music by Stephen Sondheim

TEMPO: Moderate    RHYTHM: Rhumba    COLOR: Guitar

Is-n't it rich? Are we a pair? Me here at last on the ground, you in mid-air? Send in the clowns. Is-n't it

Send In the Clowns

100

# TOMORROW

From *Annie*    Words by Martin Charnin; Music by Charles Strouse

TEMPO: Medium fast    RHYTHM: Pops    COLOR: Clarinet

## 105
### ALL THE WAY
"All the Way" went all the way to Best Film Song of 1957 and a million-selling recording for Frank Sinatra. Sammy Cahn and Jimmy Van Heusen wrote it for Sinatra to sing in *The Joker Is Wild*, the life story of Joe E. Lewis.

## 108
### AS TIME GOES BY
Oh, come on. You *must* remember this. Morocco, 1941. Rick's Café Américain. Bergman and Bogart, and Dooley Wilson playing "As Time Goes By." Movies don't come any better than *Casablanca*, and songs don't come any better than this one.

## 110
### BORN FREE
John Barry is best known for his brassy, rhythmic scores for such James Bond films as *Goldfinger* and *Thunderball*. He proved he could write softer stuff when he composed this sweeping Oscar-winning theme for *Born Free* (1966), a tremendous hit for pianist Roger Williams.

## 112
### WHEN YOU WISH UPON A STAR
It's trivia time! Who sang this Academy Award-winning song in Walt Disney's *Pinocchio* in 1940? Give up? It was Jiminy Cricket, with a voice supplied by Cliff "Ukulele Ike" Edwards, a vaudeville star of the 1920s.

## 114
### THREE COINS IN THE FOUNTAIN
Romance in Rome was the theme of *Three Coins in the Fountain*, and Sammy Cahn and Jule Styne came up with the perfect title song (an Oscar-winner) for the 1954 film. The "fountain" is the Fontana di Trevi. Legend has it that anyone who throws a coin into its waters is bound to return to the Eternal City. Try it and see.

## 116
### DAYS OF WINE AND ROSES
It's a sad story, more about wine than roses. But the 1962 movie, starring Jack Lemmon and Lee Remick, will be remembered forever, thanks in part to Henry Mancini and Johnny Mercer's bittersweet Oscar-winning title theme.

## 118
### I ONLY HAVE EYES FOR YOU
Harry Warren and Al Dubin wrote many film scores together—*42nd Street*, *Gold Diggers of 1933* and *Dames* among them—all containing many wonderful songs. Dick Powell sang "I Only Have Eyes for You" to Ruby Keeler in *Dames* (1934).

## 120
### THE GLORY OF LOVE
Boston-born Billy Hill is known for his cowboy tunes—"The Last Roundup," "Wagon Wheels" and "Empty Saddles" among them—but his Eastern upbringing came through on "The Glory of Love." The song first became popular in 1936, hit again in 1967 after it it was used in *Guess Who's Coming to Dinner*, and yet again in 1989 when Bette Midler sang it in *Beaches*.

## 122
### IT'S MAGIC
Doris Day made her reputation as a big-band singer with Les Brown and His Orchestra. Sammy Cahn and Jule Styne suggested her for a role in *Romance on the High Seas* (1948), in which she sang the composers' magical "It's Magic," and the rest is Hollywood history.

## 124
### THEME FROM *A SUMMER PLACE*
Max Steiner's theme was the best thing about the soapy *A Summer Place* (1959). It became a best-selling recording for Percy Faith and His Orchestra—a recording that is to summer what Bing Crosby's "White Christmas" is to Christmas.

## 126
### SEPTEMBER IN THE RAIN
Those leaves of brown have been tumbling down since 1937, when singer James Melton sang this lovely song in *Melody for Two*. It's another in the series of film tunes by the team of Harry Warren and Al Dubin.

## 128
### THE WAY WE WERE
Just remember: We're not getting older, we're getting better. But it's always fun to look back on the way we were. Alan and Marilyn Bergman and Marvin Hamlisch's fond glance at the past, the title song of the Barbra Streisand–Robert Redford film, won an Oscar as Best Song of the Year in 1973.

## 131
### THAT'S ALL
Among the records New York disc jockey–songwriter Bob Haymes played on his show was one of a melody he had written, called "C'est Tout." A fan call from Nat King Cole prompted Haymes to ask his friend Alan Brandt to supply lyrics for the tune. The result was this fine song, a fine recording for Cole and a fine addition to *Tootsie* 30 years later, in 1982.

# ALL THE WAY

From *The Joker Is Wild*   Words by Sammy Cahn; Music by Jimmy Van Heusen

TEMPO: Slow   RHYTHM: Bossa Nova, Pops   COLOR: Piano, Strings

All the Way

# AS TIME GOES BY

From *Casablanca*    Words and Music by Herman Hupfeld

Slow and sentimental

TEMPO: Slow    RHYTHM: Big Band, Swing    COLOR: Sax, Piano

# When you wish upon a star

From *Pinocchio*  Words by Ned Washington; Music by Leigh Harline

TEMPO: Slow  RHYTHM: 16 beat  COLOR: Strings

# Three Coins in the Fountain

From *Three Coins in the Fountain*    Words by Sammy Cahn; Music by Jule Styne

TEMPO: Moderate    RHYTHM: Bossa Nova    COLOR: Oboe, Strings

Three coins in the foun-tain, each one seek-ing hap-pi-ness,

thrown by three hope-ful lov-ers, which one will the foun-tain bless?

Three hearts in the foun-tain, each heart long-ing for its home;

There they lie in the foun-tain, some-where in the heart of Rome.

*From Days of Wine and Roses*  Words by Johnny Mercer; Music by Henry Mancini

TEMPO: Moderate  RHYTHM: Rhumba, Beguine  COLOR: Strings

**Moderate Ballad**

116

# I ONLY HAVE EYES FOR YOU

From *Dames*    Words by Al Dubin; Music by Harry Warren

TEMPO: Moderate    RHYTHM: Rhumba (Beguine)    COLOR: Strings

# THE GLORY OF LOVE

From *Guess Who's Coming to Dinner*  Words and Music by William Hill

TEMPO: Moderate  RHYTHM: Swing, Big Band  COLOR: Trumpet, Sax, Jazz Organ

# IT'S MAGIC

From *Romance on the High Seas*  Words by Sammy Cahn; Music by Jule Styne

TEMPO: Slow   RHYTHM: Bossa Nova   COLOR: Flute, Piano

Slowly

You sigh, the song be-gins, you speak and I hear vi-o-lins, it's mag - ic.

The stars de - sert the skies and rush to nes-tle in your eyes, it's

mag - ic. With-out a gold-en wand or mys-tic charms,

fan - tas-tic things be-gin when I am in your arms.

# THEME FROM A SUMMER PLACE

Words by Mack Discant; Music by Max Steiner

TEMPO: Slow    RHYTHM: Rock and Roll No. 1    COLOR: Strings

# September in the Rain

From *Melody for Two*　　　　Words by Al Dubin; Music by Harry Warren

TEMPO: Moderate　　RHYTHM: Swing, Bossa Nova　　COLOR: Brass Ensemble

# THE WAY WE WERE

From *The Way We Were*   Words by Alan and Marilyn Bergman; Music by Marvin Hamlisch

TEMPO: Slow   RHYTHM: Disco, 16 beat   COLOR: Piano, Organ

The Way We Were

F Am F E(7) Am
may be beau-ti-ful and yet, what's so pain-ful to re-mem - ber
F Am Am/G bass F Em7 E7 Am Am/G
F E Am F Em
we sim-ply choose to for - get. So it's the laugh - ter
F E7 Am Am/G bass F Em
F Em F Em
we will re - mem - ber, when-ev-er we re - mem - ber
F Em F Em
F C Fm C
the way we were, the way we were.
F Dm7/G C Gm/B♭ A7 Fm/A♭ Cmaj7

# That's All

From *Tootsie*    Words and Music by Alan Brandt and Bob Haymes
TEMPO: Slow   RHYTHM: Pops, Big Band   COLOR: Strings, Piano

Very slowly, with expression

I can on-ly give you love that lasts for-ev-er and the
prom-ise to be near each time you call, and the on-ly heart I own for
you and you a-lone, that's all, that's all. I can

That's All

### 135
### I DON'T KNOW WHY (I JUST DO)

In 1931, the great songwriting team of Fred Ahlert and Roy Turk turned out "Where the Blue of the Night (Meets the Gold of the Day)," which Bing Crosby co-wrote and made his theme song, and "I Don't Know Why"—which sparkled even brighter and oftener because *everybody* sang it.

### 136
### MEAN TO ME

Here's another hit by Ahlert and Turk. Written in 1929, it was one of the last great torch songs of the '20s. Not surprisingly, it was a hit for the two great torch singers of the period, Helen Morgan and Ruth Etting.

### 138
### YOU MADE ME LOVE YOU

Songwriters Joe McCarthy and James Monaco made us love this song—ever since 1913, when Al Jolson introduced it on Broadway. Judy Garland sang it in *Broadway Melody of 1938*, and Harry James recorded it in 1941, with hints of both Jolson and Garland in his trumpet phrasing.

### 140
### FOR ME AND MY GAL

Songwriters can be businessmen too, you know. When George W. Meyer was asked why he composed "For Me and My Gal" in 1917 (along with Edgar Leslie and E. Ray Goetz), he answered, "I was writing songs for a living and I needed the money." By the way, lyricist Leslie borrowed the title from the last line of another golden oldie, "Shine On, Harvest Moon."

### 142
### DANNY BOY

Here's a song that has brought a tear to many an eye—and not just Irish ones. The melody became known as "Londonderry Air" after it appeared in print for the first time in 1855 in a collection put together by a Miss J. Ross of Londonderry. It wasn't until 1912 that Fred E. Weatherly gave the air the words that made it "Danny Boy."

### 144
### SIDE BY SIDE

Duos—of singers, comedians, dancers—have been performing "Side by Side" ever since Harry Woods wrote it in 1927. Kay Starr followed the trend when she made her hit recording in 1953. Her partner? Herself: she overdubbed her own voice.

### 146
### MY BLUE HEAVEN

Composer Walter Donaldson was a bachelor when he and George Whiting wrote this paean to married life in 1927. The tune was a tremendous hit for singer Gene Austin that same year. The modest Austin once said: "The most important element in the success of a record is the song, not the singer. I got an old sayin': 'Hit songs don't care who sings 'em.' "

### 148
### MY BUDDY

Walter Donaldson again, this time with lyricist Gus Kahn. The two clicked with this touching waltz, their first collaboration, in 1922. Realizing that they had a good thing going, they went on to create such other standards as "Carolina in the Morning," "Yes Sir, That's My Baby," "Makin' Whoopee" and "Love Me or Leave Me."

### 150
### BYE BYE BLACKBIRD

Ray Henderson and Mort Dixon's "Bye Bye Blackbird" came along in 1926. The song—a favorite of singing comedians Eddie Cantor and Georgie Price—was one of 10 hits that Henderson wrote in 1925 and 1926, among them "The Birth of the Blues," "Five Foot Two," "Alabamy Bound," "I'm Sitting on Top of the World" and "Black Bottom."

### 152
### APRIL SHOWERS

Buddy De Sylva wrote the words for three of Al Jolson's greatest hits—"Avalon," "California Here I Come" and "April Showers." Jolson introduced "April Showers" (the melody was by Louis Silvers) in the Broadway musical *Bombo* in 1921 and continued to sing it throughout his career.

### 154
### POOR BUTTERFLY

John Golden wrote the lyrics of "Poor Butterfly" in 1916, basing them on the plot of Puccini's opera *Madama Butterfly*. (Raymond Hubbell supplied the melody.) Stage star Sophye Bernard's performance of the song in *The Big Show*, an extravaganza at New York City's Hippodrome, turned the graceful ballad into one of the era's biggest hits.

### 156
### I'M LOOKING OVER A FOUR-LEAF CLOVER

Mort Dixon teamed with Harry Woods to write this happy, jaunty 1920s song. It's been a favorite of the banjo-and-mandolin bands that march in Philadelphia's annual Mummers' Parade ever since, and was a good-luck charm for bandleader Art Mooney, who copied the string bands' style for a hit recording in 1947.

### 158
### ALEXANDER'S RAGTIME BAND

Can you name five songs written by the great Irving Berlin that begin with the letter A? Hint: "Alexander's Ragtime Band" was the first one...way back in 1911. Others that you're sure to know are "All Alone," "All by Myself," "Anything You Can Do" and the immortal "Always."

### 160
### ARE YOU LONESOME TONIGHT?

What is a country song like "Are You Lonesome Tonight?" doing in a group of old-time tunes, you ask? Well, sure, Elvis Presley had a huge hit with it in 1960, but in fact the song was written back in 1926 by Tin Pan Alley veterans Roy Turk and Lou Handman, who probably had no idea what "country music" was.

### 162
### TILL WE MEET AGAIN

This charming waltz by Richard Whiting and Raymond Egan, published in 1918, was one of the hit songs of World War I. It was the first of a string of successes by composer Whiting (father of singer Margaret) that included "The Japanese Sandman," "Sleepy Time Gal" and "Beyond the Blue Horizon."

### 164
### SHINE ON, HARVEST MOON

Let's hope that vaudevillians Nora Bayes and Jack Norworth had some inkling that they were writing perhaps the ultimate singing-round-the-campfire song when they created "Shine On, Harvest Moon" in 1908. Norworth also wrote the words of another perennial seasonal favorite: "Take Me Out to the Ball Game."

### 165
### TOO-RA-LOO-RA-LOO-RAL (THAT'S AN IRISH LULLABY)

Before there was Bing Crosby (who sang "Too-Ra-Loo-Ra-Loo-Ral" to that leprechaun of a priest, Barry Fitzgerald, in *Going My Way* in 1944), there was Chauncey Olcott. Singer-songwriter Olcott specialized in sentimental Irish airs. He popularized James Royce Shannon's "Irish lullaby" (in 1914) as well as his own classics, "My Wild Irish Rose," "When Irish Eyes Are Smiling" and "Mother Machree."

# I DON'T KNOW WHY

## (I Just Do)

Words by Roy Turk; Music by Fred E. Ahlert

TEMPO: Moderately Slow   RHYTHM: Swing, Big Band   COLOR: Jazz Organ, Trombone

Words and Music by Roy Turk and Fred E. Ahlert

TEMPO: Moderate    RHYTHM: Swing, Big Band    COLOR: Trumpet, Sax

# YOU MADE ME LOVE YOU

Words by Joseph McCarthy; Music by James V. Monaco

Moderately, with a lilt ( ♩♩ played as ♩♪ )    TEMPO: Moderate    RHYTHM: Big Band, Swing    COLOR: Trumpet, Strings, Accordion

You made me love you. I did-n't want to do it; I did-n't want to do it.

You made me want you, and all the time you knew it; I guess you al-ways knew it.

You made me hap-py; Some-times you made me glad. But there were

times, dear, you made me feel so bad. You made me

138

# For Me and My Gal

Words by Edgar Leslie and E. Ray Goetz; Music by George W. Meyer

TEMPO: Moderate   RHYTHM: Swing   COLOR: Strings

140

# DANNY BOY

Words by Fred E. Weatherly; Music Traditional

TEMPO: Moderate  RHYTHM: Rhumba or Swing  COLOR: Flute, Strings

# SIDE BY SIDE

Words and Music by Harry Woods

Moderately ( ♫ played as ᴛ³♪ )　　　TEMPO: Moderate　RHYTHM: Big Band, Swing　COLOR: Banjo, Honkytonk Piano

Oh, we ain't got a bar-rel of mon-ey, may-be we're rag-ged and fun-ny, but we'll trav-el a-long sing-in' a song side by side.

Don't know what's com-in' to-mor-row, may-be it's trou-ble and sor-row, but we'll trav-el the road shar-in' our load side by side.

Words by George Whiting; Music by Walter Donaldson

TEMPO: Moderately fast   RHYTHM: Big Band   COLOR: Trumpet, Clarinet, Sax

Nice and easy

# My Buddy

Words by Gus Kahn; Music by Walter Donaldson

TEMPO: Moderately slow   RHYTHM: Waltz   COLOR: Music Box, Violin, Vibraphone

\* For a charming "music box" effect, play both hands an 8va higher.

# Bye Bye Blackbird

Words by Mort Dixon; Music by Roy Henderson

Moderate singalong tempo     TEMPO: Moderate     RHYTHM: Big Band, Swing     COLOR: Trumpet, Clarinet, Trombone, Jazz Organ

# April Showers

Words by B.G. DeSylva; Music by Louis Silvers

TEMPO: Moderate   RHYTHM: Big Band, Swing   COLOR: Strings, Clarinet

# POOR BUTTERFLY

Words by John L. Golden; Music by Raymond Hubbell

Moderately slow

TEMPO: Moderately slow   RHYTHM: Swing, Rhumba   COLOR: Strings, Flute

154

# I'm Looking Over a Four-Leaf Clover

Words by Mort Dixon; Music by Harry Woods

TEMPO: Fast   RHYTHM: Big Band, Swing   COLOR: Trumpet, Banjo

# ALEXANDER'S RAGTIME BAND

Words and Music by Irving Berlin

Moderate swing

TEMPO: Moderately fast  RHYTHM: Swing, Big Band  COLOR: Sax, Jazz Organ

158

# Are You Lonesome Tonight?

Words and Music by Roy Turk and Lou Handman

TEMPO: Moderate   RHYTHM: Waltz   COLOR: Organ, Strings

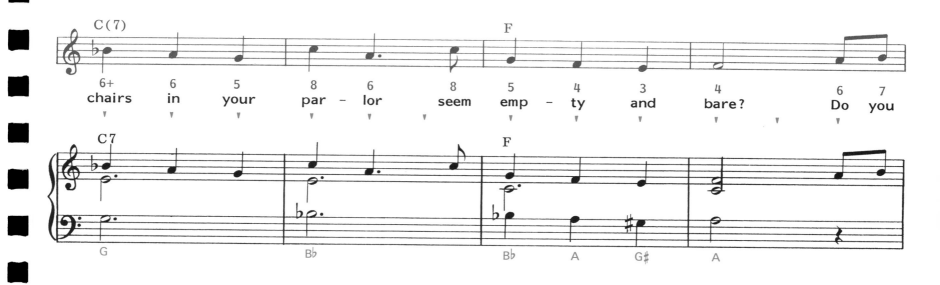

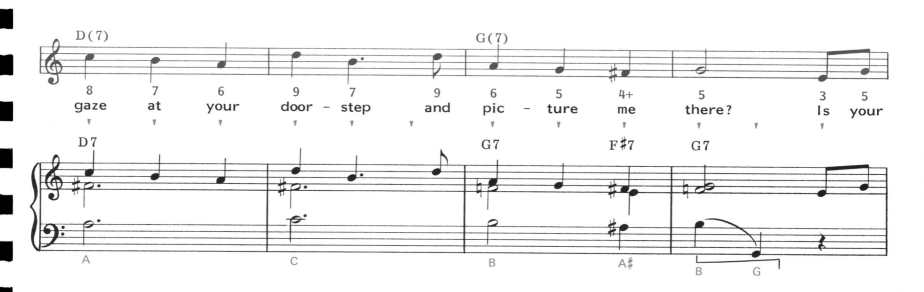

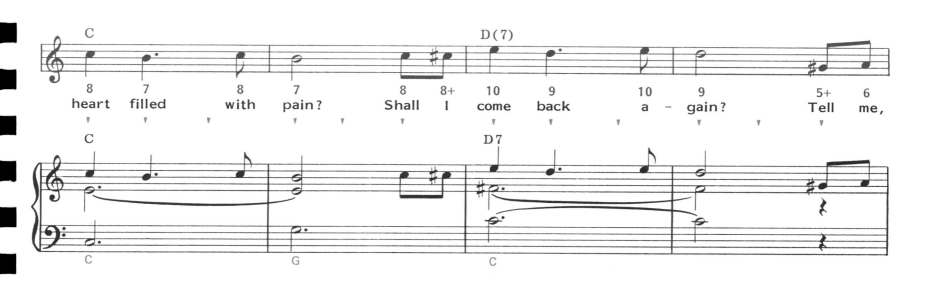

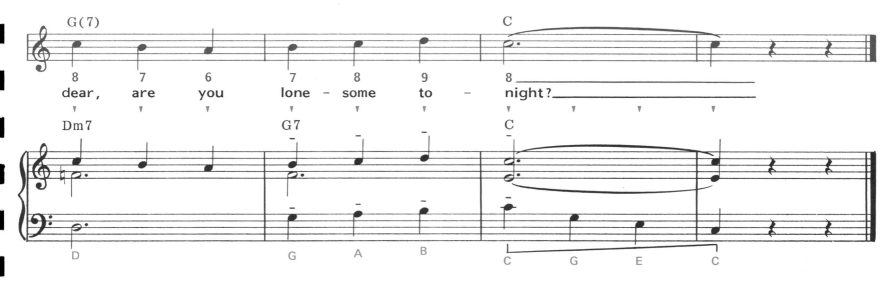

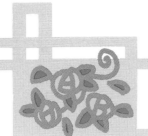

# TILL WE MEET AGAIN

Words by Raymond Egan; Music by Richard Whiting

TEMPO: Slow to moderate    RHYTHM: Waltz    COLOR: Strings, Harmonica or Accordion

Slow waltz

Smile the while you kiss me sad a – dieu,

when the clouds roll by I'll come to you;

Then the skies will seem more blue

down in lov – ers' lane, my dear – ie.

# SHINE ON, HARVEST MOON

Words and Music by Nora Bayes and Jack Norworth

TEMPO: Moderate   RHYTHM: Big Band, Swing   COLOR: Banjo, Harmonica

# TOO-RA-LOO-RA-LOO-RAL

**(That's an Irish Lullaby)**

Words and Music by James Royce Shannon

TEMPO: Moderate   RHYTHM: Disco   COLOR: Panpipe, Flute

Moderately, with expression

### 167
### AMAZING GRACE

John Newton's poem, written as part of a sermon in 1779, has become one of the most popular hymns of all time. Newton, by that time an ordained minister in the Anglican church, had been captain of a slave ship for many years—and was rescued from that life by the power of grace.

### 168
### HOW GREAT THOU ART

Although it dates back more than 100 years, "How Great Thou Art" is one of the most recent—and most popular—of religious songs. It was written in 1886 by a Swedish missionary, but was not translated into English until 1948, by the Reverend Stuart K. Hine. It became popular in the 1950s, thanks to George Beverly Shea, who sang it often during the Billy Graham Crusades.

### 170
### WHISPERING HOPE

We're indebted to Philadelphian Septimus Winner for such odes as "Where Oh Where Has My Little Dog Gone," "Listen to the Mocking Bird," "What Is Home Without a Mother?" and—in a more tranquil vein—"Whispering Hope." He published "Whispering Hope" in 1868, under his mother's maiden name, Alice Hawthorne, presumably thinking the song's tender sentiments more feminine than masculine.

### 172
### ROCK OF AGES

Augustus Toplady's beloved hymn "Rock of Ages," written in 1776, has consistently been among the top five favorite gospel songs. It was set to its present tune by the American composer and teacher Thomas Hastings in 1832.

### 173
### PRAISE GOD FROM WHOM ALL BLESSINGS FLOW

Thomas Ken, an Anglican bishop, was royal chaplain to one British king, prisoner in the Tower of London of another. He will always be remembered for this simple four-line stanza, which he wrote in 1674 for a prayer manual. The sturdy tune it is set to, called "Old Hundredth," was composed by Louis Bourgeois and published in 1551.

### 174
### IN THE GARDEN

In 1912, C. Austin Miles experienced a spiritual vision in which he saw Mary Magdalene and Jesus in the Garden of Gethsemane, where Jesus was buried. Miles awoke from his trance inspired to write the poem for this timeless gospel favorite. He added the music that night.

### 175
### SHENANDOAH

Was "Shenandoah" named for a river in Virginia, a valley, an Indian maid or an Indian chief? The origins of the haunting song are clouded by time. Over the past two centuries, different versions of it have been sung by lumberjacks, river-barge men and sailors on the original tall ships. Our thanks to all of them.

### 176
### GOODNIGHT, IRENE

Huddie Ledbetter, or Leadbelly, the legendary singer-guitarist from Louisiana, learned "Goodnight, Irene" from his uncle. He had been singing it for years when he first recorded it, for a Library of Congress folk-song project, in 1933. Leadbelly always believed the song could become a hit. He died in 1949, a year before The Weavers' recording became just that.

### 178
### GREENSLEEVES

Legend has it that the oft-married English king Henry VIII wrote "Greensleeves." Whether he did or not, it's a regal tune. At Christmastime, the hymn "What Child Is This?" is sung to the melody.

### 180
### I CAN'T STOP LOVING YOU

Many Nashville songwriters strive for years to come up with a hit song; Don Gibson managed to write two country classics in one afternoon: "I Can't Stop Loving You" and "Oh, Lonesome Me." The songs provided Gibson with a double-sided No.1 hit in 1958. "I Can't Stop Loving You" was also a big success for another country singer, Kitty Wells, and for rhythm-and-blues star Ray Charles.

### 182
### TENNESSEE WALTZ

Pee Wee King and Redd Stewart's "Tennessee Waltz" was one of the first country and western songs to become a pop music hit, thanks to Patti Page's 1950 recording. Even though it's about a broken romance, not about the virtues of Tennessee, the ballad is now the official song of the Volunteer State.

### 184
### DON'T FENCE ME IN

Guess who takes credit for this tune of the wide-open spaces? None other than Yale man Cole Porter, one of the most sophisticated of composers. For the lyrics, though, Porter turned to a poem he had bought in the 1930s from a genuine rider of the purple sage—for $200.

# AMAZING GRACE

*Words by John Newton; Music Traditional*

TEMPO: Moderate   RHYTHM: None (Use single finger bass)   COLOR: Bagpipe, Oboe
*Note: If you have the Bagpipe sound on your keyboard, hold down the F and C keys with the left hand and play the melody with the right hand.*

*Additional Verses*

How sweet the name of Jesus sounds
In a believer's ear;
It soothes his sorrows, heals his wounds,
And drives away his fear.

Must Jesus bear the cross alone
And all the world go free?
No, there's a cross for ev'ryone,
And there's a cross for me.

# How Great Thou Art

English Words by Stuart K. Hine; Swedish Folk Melody

Slowly, with reverence    TEMPO: Moderately slow and stately    RHYTHM: None, play freely    COLOR: Pipe Organ

1. O Lord, my God, when I in awe-some won - der_____ con - sid - er
2. When through the woods and for - est glades I wan - der_____ and hear the

(1) all the worlds Thy hands have made;_____ I see the stars, I hear the roll - ing
(2) birds sing sweet - ly in the trees;_____ When I look down from loft - y moun - tain

(1) thun - der,_____ Thy pow'r through-out the u - ni - verse dis - played._____
(2) gran - deur_____ and hear the brook and feel the gen - tle breeze._____

*Additional Verses*

And when I think that God, His Son not sparing,
Sent Him to die, I scarce can take it in;
That on the cross my burden gladly bearing,
He bled and died to take away my sin.
*(Repeat Chorus)*

When Christ shall come with shout of acclamation
And take me home, what joy shall fill my heart.
Then I shall bow in humble adoration
And there proclaim, my God, how great Thou art!
*(Repeat Chorus)*

# Whispering Hope

Words and Music by Alice Hawthorne

Moderate waltz

TEMPO: Moderate   RHYTHM: Waltz (or none)   COLOR: Organ, Human Voice (Vox Humana)

Soft as the voice of an an-gel breath-ing a les-son un-heard;_____ Hope with a gen-tle per-sua-sion whis-pers her com-fort-ing word:_____ Wait till the dark-ness is o-ver, wait till the tem-pest is done;_____

170

※ *The last 16 measures are played twice.*

# ROCK OF AGES

Words by Augustus M. Toplady; Music by Thomas Hastings

TEMPO: Moderately slow   RHYTHM: Waltz (or none)   COLOR: Organ

1. Rock of A - ges, cleft for me! Let me hide my - self in
2. Could my tears for - ev - er flow, could my zeal no lan - guor

(1) Thee; Let the wa - ter and the blood from Thy wound - ed side which
(2) know, Let these for sin could not a - tone; Thou must save and Thou a -

(1) flowed, be of sin the dou - ble cure: Save from wrath and make me pure.
(2) lone. In my hand no price I bring, sim - ply to Thy cross I cling.

Repeat from the beginning

# Praise God from Whom All Blessings Flow

Words by Thomas Ken; Music by Louis Bourgeois

TEMPO: Slow and stately   RHYTHM: None   COLOR: Organ

# IN THE GARDEN

Words and Music by C. Austin Miles

Very slowly in 2 (♩.= 1 beat)
or Moderately in 6 (♪ = 1 beat)

TEMPO: Slow    RHYTHM: Slow Gospel (Rock and Roll)    COLOR: Organ

1. I come to the gar-den a-lone, while the dew is still on the ros-es; And the
2. He speaks, and the sound of His voice is so sweet the birds hush their sing-ing; And the
3. I'd stay in the gar-den with Him though the night a-round me be fall-ing; But He

(1) voice I hear fall-ing on my ear, the Son of God dis-clos-es.
(2) mel-o-dy that He gave to me with-in my heart is ring-ing.  } And He
(3) bids me go; Through the voice of woe, His voice to me is call-ing.

walks with me, and He talks with me, and He tells me I am His own; And the

joy we share as we tar-ry there, none oth-er has ev-er known.

# SHENANDOAH

Traditional

Freely

TEMPO: Slow  RHYTHM: None, play freely  COLOR: Harmonica, Oboe

1. Oh, Shen-an-doah,_____ I long to hear you,
2. Oh, Shen-an-doah,_____ I love your daugh-ter,  } A - way, you roll-ing
3. Oh, Shen-an-doah,_____ I'm goin' to leave you,

(1) { Oh, Shen-an-doah,_____ just to be near you,
riv - er. (2) { Oh, Shen-an-doah,_____ a-cross the wa-ter,  } A - way, we're bound a-
(3) { Oh, Shen-an-doah,_____ I won't de - ceive you,

way, 'cross the wide Mis - sou - ri.

*Repeat from the beginning for additional words.*

# Goodnight, Irene

Words and Music by Huddie Ledbetter and John Lomax

TEMPO: Moderate   RHYTHM: Waltz   COLOR: Harmonica, Guitar

Moderate waltz

Chorus

I - rene, good - night; I - rene, good - night. Good - night, I - rene; Good - night, I - rene; I'll see you in my dreams.

Last time end here

last time, slower

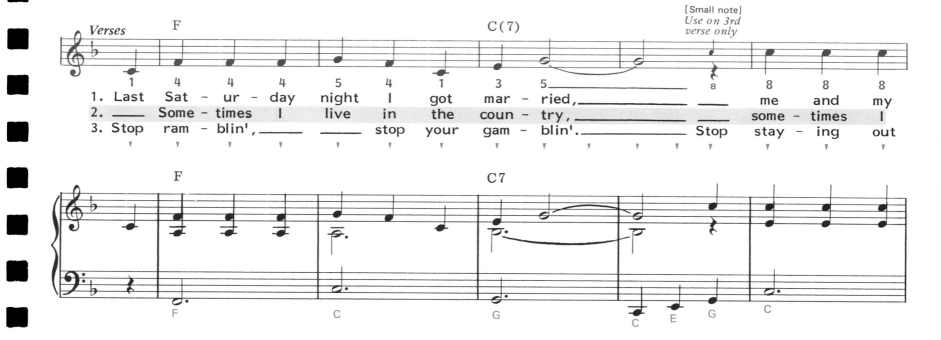

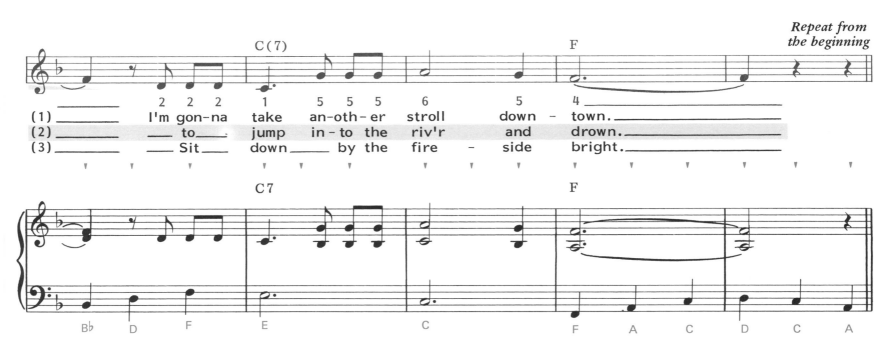

# GREENSLEEVES

Traditional

TEMPO: Moderate   RHYTHM: Waltz   COLOR: Recorder, Pan Flute

# I CAN'T STOP LOVING YOU

Words and Music by Don Gibson

Moderately

TEMPO: Moderate   RHYTHM: Country   COLOR: Strings, Rock Organ

Those hap-py hours that we once knew, though long a - go still make me blue. They say that time heals a bro-ken heart, but time has stood still since we've been a - part.

* This song begins on the 2nd beat of the measure.

# Tennessee Waltz

Words and Music by Redd Stewart and Pee Wee King

Moderately slow waltz

TEMPO: Moderately slow    RHYTHM: Waltz    COLOR: Strings, Electric Guitar

# Don't Fence Me In

Words and Music by Cole Porter

TEMPO: Moderately slow  RHYTHM: Country or Swing  COLOR: Banjo, Guitar

Loping along

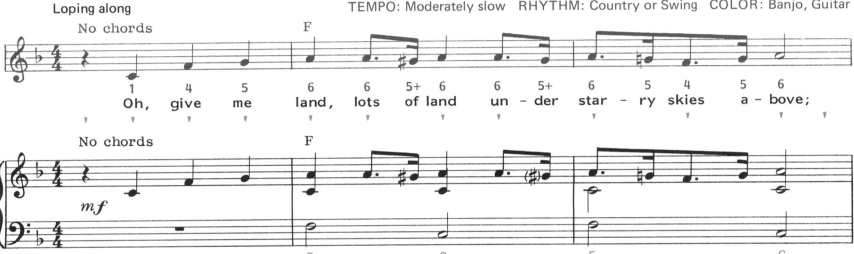

Oh, give me land, lots of land un-der star-ry skies a-bove;

Don't fence me in. Let me ride through the wide o-pen

coun-try that I love; Don't fence me in. Let me

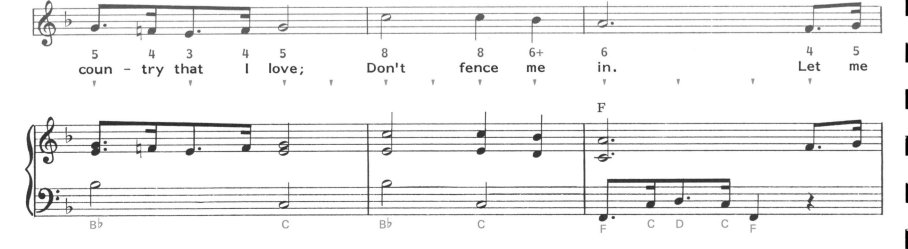

Don't Fence Me In

188
### GOD BLESS AMERICA

You know, "The Star-Spangled Banner" didn't officially become the national anthem of the United States until 1931. And if there's ever a referendum to replace it, one of the chief contenders will surely be Irving Berlin's hymn to his adopted country. The Russian-born composer never profited from this enduring classic. He donated all the royalties to the Boy Scouts and Girl Scouts of America.

190
### AMERICA THE BEAUTIFUL

Katherine Lee Bates's "America the Beautiful" was a runner-up for U.S. national anthem back in 1931. Miss Bates was a professor of English who had been to Europe several times but hadn't seen much of her own country. When she made her first trip west, in 1893, she was awed by the view from the top of Pikes Peak in Colorado. She promptly wrote this stirring hymn of praise, which she elected to set to a stately tune by Samuel A. Ward.

191
### THIS LAND IS YOUR LAND

In a sense, nobody ever really wrote this melody. Wandering minstrel Woody Guthrie adapted the music from two songs by the Carter Family, who in turn had borrowed the tune from an even older folk song. "This Land Is Your Land" was introduced by The Weavers in 1956 and helped to fire the folk music revival that soon followed.

192
### DIXIE

"Dixie" has been a rallying cry for the South from Civil War days to the present, but the song was written by a Yankee, Ohio-born minstrel man Dan Emmett. In 1859, Emmett was performing with a troupe in New York City. As he sat in his boardinghouse one cold, rainy Sunday, trying to write a closing song for the show, the dismal weather made him wish he were "in the land of cotton." The rest is part of history.

194
### BATTLE HYMN OF THE REPUBLIC

The Northern equivalent of "Dixie" during the Civil War was the work of Julia Ward Howe, a poet, abolitionist and suffragette. She wrote "Battle Hymn of the Republic"—to the same tune as "John Brown's Body"—after touring an army camp near Washington, D.C., in 1861. Her poem was published the following year in the *Atlantic Monthly*, and has been a source of inspiration ever since.

196
### ANNIVERSARY SONG

Written in 1880 by Romanian composer Ion Ivanovici, "Danube Waves" has long been a favorite at Jewish weddings. In 1947, Al Jolson and Saul Chaplin tried to capture that atmosphere for the film *The Jolson Story* and turned "Danube Waves" into "Anniversary Song." Larry Parks played the "world's greatest entertainer" on-screen, but Jolson did his own singing on the soundtrack. His recording of "Anniversary Song" became a best-seller.

198
### LET ME CALL YOU SWEETHEART

Leo Friedman and Beth Slater Whitson made a mistake with their first song: in 1909 they sold "Meet Me Tonight in Dreamland" outright to the publisher. They got a few dollars; the publisher reaped a fortune when the tune sold more than 2 million copies of sheet music. The composers struck a better bargain the following year for "Let Me Call You Sweetheart": this time they got royalties on the 5 million copies sold.

200
### RUDOLPH THE RED-NOSED REINDEER

Robert L. May, a copywriter for Montgomery Ward, wrote a little story about a reindeer with a bright red nose in 1939. Ten years later, songwriter Johnny Marks took the tale of Rudolph and created a Christmas classic. Singing cowboy Gene Autry's 1949 recording sold more than 2 million copies.

202
### WINTER WONDERLAND

Richard Smith and Felix Bernard wrote this cozy ballad about the wonders of wintertime in 1934, but it wasn't until 1950 that the song became popular, thanks to a recording by The Andrews Sisters. Since then, it's been a perennial favorite.

204
### AULD LANG SYNE

Scottish poet Robert Burns created this hymn to "old long ago" in the late 18th century. For 150 years, it was simply a song of the parting of friends. Then, on New Year's Eve in 1929, Guy Lombardo decided to play it at midnight. The song became so associated with New Year's Eve and with Lombardo that the bandleader used to joke: "When I go, New Year's Eve goes with me." It hasn't been the same without him.

205
### HAPPY DAYS ARE HERE AGAIN

"Happy Days Are Here Again" is one of the first Depression-era songs, although it was written early in 1929, before the stock market crash in October. Its use was ironic, but it helped to lift spirits in those grim years and became Franklin D. Roosevelt's campaign song in 1932. Barbra Streisand took it up and made it a hit again in 1963.

208
### HAPPY BIRTHDAY TO YOU

No, people haven't been singing "Happy Birthday to You" for hundreds of years. Sisters Patty and Mildred Hill, kindergarten teachers in Louisville, Kentucky, wrote it in 1893. Because it wasn't copyrighted until 1935, however, the song still earns royalties—up to $1 million a year. Not surprisingly, the *Guinness Book of World Records* lists it as one of the three most popular songs in the English language (along with "Auld Lang Syne" and "For He's a Jolly Good Fellow").

# GOD BLESS AMERICA

Words and Music by Irving Berlin

TEMPO: Moderately slow   RHYTHM: March   COLOR: Brass Ensemble, Strings, Organ

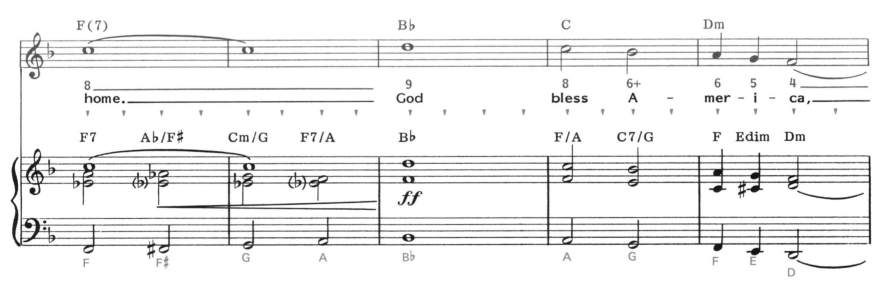

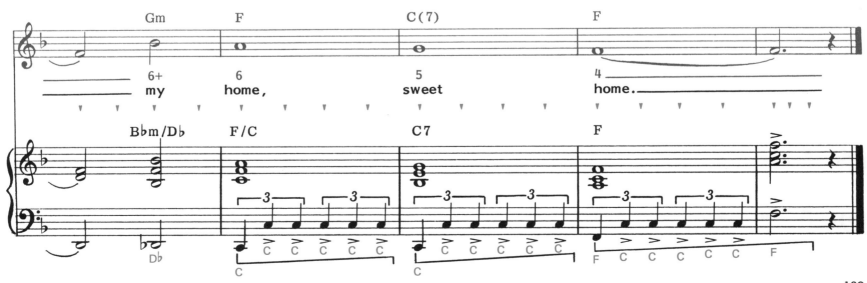

# America the Beautiful

Words by Katherine Lee Bates; Music by Samuel Augustus Ward

TEMPO: Moderate    RHYTHM: None (or very slow march)    COLOR: Organ

Moderately

1. O beau-ti-ful for spa-cious skies, for am-ber waves of grain, for
2. O beau-ti-ful for pil-grim feet, whose stern im-pas-sioned stress, a
3. O beau-ti-ful for pa-triot dream that sees be-yond the years, thine

(1) pur-ple moun-tain maj-es-ties a-bove the fruit-ed plain. A-mer-i-ca! A-mer-i-ca! God
(2) thor-ough-fare for free-dom beat a-cross the wil-der-ness. A-mer-i-ca! A-mer-i-ca! God
(3) al-a-bas-ter ci-ties gleam un-dimmed by hu-man tears. A-mer-i-ca! A-mer-i-ca! God

(1) shed His grace on thee, and crown thy good with broth-er-hood from sea to shin-ing sea.
(2) mend thine ev-'ry flaw, con-firm thy soul in self-con-trol, thy lib-er-ty in law.
(3) shed His grace on thee, and crown thy good with broth-er-hood from sea to shin-ing sea.

# THIS LAND IS YOUR LAND

Words and Music by Woody Guthrie

TEMPO: Moderate/Very fast   RHYTHM: March/Country   COLOR: Guitar, Banjo
(Change color on each successive chorus)

With spirit

1. This land is your land, this land is my land, from Cal-i-
2. As I was walk-ing that rib-bon of high-way, I saw a-

(1) for-nia to the New York is-land. From the red-wood for-est to the Gulf Stream
(2) bove me that end-less sky-way. I saw be-low me that gold-en

(1) wa-ters, } this land was made for you and me.
(2) val-ley, }

*This song begins on the 2nd beat of the measure.

### Additional Verses

I've roamed and rambled, and I followed my footsteps
To the sparkling sands of her diamond deserts.
And all around me a voice was sounding,
This land was made for you and me.

When the sun comes shining and I was strolling,
And the wheat fields waving and the dust clouds rolling;
As the fog was lifting, a voice was chanting,
This land was made for you and me.

Words and Music by Daniel Decatur Emmett

**Spirited March**

TEMPO: Moderately slow  RHYTHM: March  COLOR: Brass Ensemble, Flute

5 3 1 1 1 2 3 4 5 5 5 3 6 6 6 5
I___ wish I was___ in the land of cot - ton, old times there are

6 5 6 7 8 9 10 8 5 8 5 3 5 2 3
not for-got-ten. Look a – way! Look a – way! Look a – way, Dix – ie

1 5 3 1 1 1 2 3 4 5 5 5 3 6 6 6 5
Land. In___ Dix – ie Land___ where___ I was born in ear - ly on one

6 5 6 7 8 9 10 8 5 8 5 3 5 2 3 1 5 5
frost – y morn-in'. Look a – way! Look a – way! Look a – way, Dix-ie Land. Then I

# BATTLE HYMN OF THE REPUBLIC

Words by Julia Ward Howe; Music by William Steffe

Moderately slow march    TEMPO: Moderately slow    RHYTHM: March or without rhythm    COLOR: Organ, Brass Choir, Trumpet
(repeat chord on each beat)

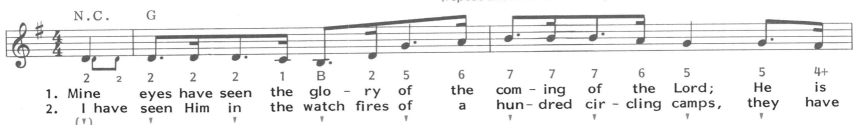

1. Mine eyes have seen the glo - ry of the com - ing of the Lord; He is
2. I have seen Him in the watch fires of a hun - dred cir - cling camps, they have

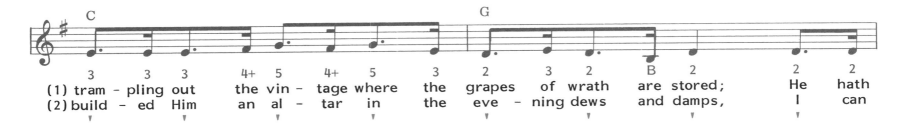

(1) tram - pling out the vin - tage where the grapes of wrath are stored; He hath
(2) build - ed Him an al - tar in the eve - ning dews and damps, I can

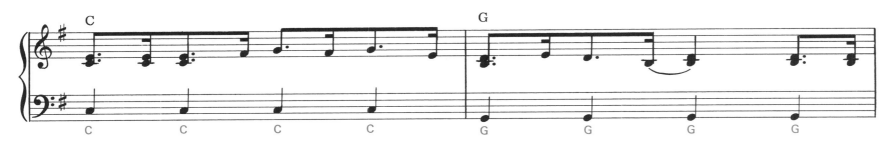

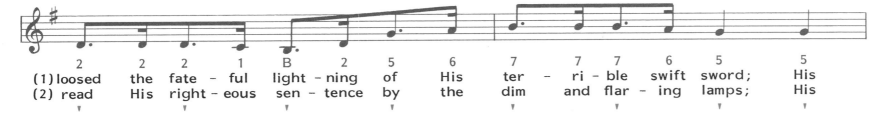

(1) loosed the fate - ful light - ning of His ter - ri - ble swift sword; His
(2) read His right - eous sen - tence by the dim and flar - ing lamps; His

### Additional Verses

He has sounded forth the trumpet that shall never sound retreat;
He is sifting out the hearts of men before His judgment seat;
O be swift, my soul, to answer Him! Be jubilant, my feet!
Our God is marching on.
*(Chorus)*

In the beauty of the lilies, Christ was born across the sea,
With a glory in His bosom that transfigures you and me.
As He died to make men holy, let us die to make men free,
While God is marching on.
*(Chorus)*

# ANNIVERSARY SONG

Words by Al Jolson; Music by Saul Chaplin

TEMPO: Moderate   RHYTHM: Waltz   COLOR: Strings, Cello

1. Oh, how we danced on the night we were wed; We vowed our true love though a word was not said. The world was in bloom, there were stars in the skies,

(2) night seemed to fade into blossoming dawn, the sun shone anew but the dance lingered on. Could we but relive that sweet moment sublime, we'd

*Repeat from the beginning and play through to the word "Fine." Use the second set of words.*

197

# LET ME CALL YOU SWEETHEART

Words by Beth Slater Whitson; Music by Leo Friedman

TEMPO: Moderate   RHYTHM: Waltz   COLOR: Strings, Organ

# RUDOLPH THE RED-NOSED REINDEER

Words and Music by Johnny Marks

Moderately

TEMPO: Moderate to Fast    RHYTHM: Country or Swing    COLOR: Toy or Electric Piano, Vibraphone

# WINTER WONDERLAND

Words by Richard Smith; Music by Felix Bernard

TEMPO: Moderate   RHYTHM: Big Band, Swing   COLOR: Strings, Accordion, Guitar

Sleigh bells ring; Are you list-'nin'? In the lane, snow is glis-t'nin', a beau-ti-ful sight,___ we're hap-py to-night ___ walk-in' in a win-ter won-der-land. Gone a-way is the blue-bird, here to stay is a new bird; He sings a love song___ as we go a-long,___ walk-in' in a win-ter won-der-land.

202

# Auld Lang Syne

Words by Robert Burns; Music Traditional

TEMPO: Moderately  RHYTHM: None, or March  COLOR: Brass Choir, Organ or Bagpipe

Should auld ac-quaint-ance be for-got and nev-er brought to mind? Should

auld ac-quaint-ance be for-got and days of auld lang syne. For

auld___ lang___ syne, my dear, for auld___ lang___ syne; We'll

take a cup of kind-ness yet for auld___ lang___ syne.

# Happy Days Are Here Again

Words by Jack Yellen; Music by Milton Ager

**With a lift**

TEMPO: Fast   RHYTHM: March/Polka   COLOR: Trumpet, Brass Ensemble

Happy Days Are Here Again

# Happy Birthday to you

Words and Music by Mildred J. Hill and Patty Smith Hill

TEMPO: Moderate   RHYTHM: Waltz   COLOR: Piano, Accordion